Be Effective on LinkedIn®

With #TheLinkedInGuru

Jeff Young

Copyright © 2024 by Jeff Young

All rights reserved.

No portion of this book may be reproduced in any form without written permission from the publisher or author, except as permitted by U.S. copyright law.

ISBN: 9798337768908

rev p20240829.B.002

Disclaimers

LinkedIn is the registered trademark of LinkedIn Corporation or its affiliates. The use of the LinkedIn trademark in connection with this product does not signify any affiliation with or endorsement by LinkedIn Corporation or its affiliates.

Jeff Young (aka #TheLinkedInGuru) does not work for and is not in any way associated with LinkedIn® or Microsoft.

Contents

Foreword	VII
Introduction	1
1. Getting Started - The Foundations of LinkedIn® Success	5
2. Optimizing Your LinkedIn® Profile	9
3. Building Your Network	13
4. Content Creation and Engagement	19
5. Advanced LinkedIn® Techniques	25
6. LinkedIn® for Specific Goals	31
7. Measuring Your LinkedIn® Success	37
8. Staying Up-to-Date with LinkedIn®	43
9. Common Mistakes to Avoid on LinkedIn®	49
10. Conclusion - Your LinkedIn® Journey Continues	55
11. Appendices	61
About the Author	67
Acknowledgments	69

Foreword

I volunteered to write the foreword for this book because I was filled with excitement and a deep sense of purpose. As a Livestream & Author Brand Strategist, I've had the privilege of collaborating with many industry experts, but Jeff Young stands out in a league of his own.

This book is more than just a guide to LinkedIn® - it's a labor of love and tribute to a man who has tirelessly dedicated himself to helping others succeed on this powerful platform. As Chief Collaborator on this project, I've had the unique opportunity to distill Jeff's years of wisdom and experience into these pages, and it's been an incredible journey.

Jeff Young, affectionately known as #TheLinkedInGuru, is a fixture in the LinkedIn® community. Day in and day out, he's there, supporting thousands of people – from newbies to veterans, job seekers to entrepreneurs, small businesses to large corporations. And the most remarkable part? Jeff does it all for free, jokingly saying he likes to get paid in chocolate.

I've had the pleasure of collaborating with Jeff in numerous ways over the years. He's been a guest on my LinkedIn® Lives multiple times, bringing his infectious energy and wealth of knowledge to my show. We've co-authored document posts and worked together on several LinkedIn® newsletters. Each collaboration has been an absolute delight.

But this book? This is the ultimate honor. It's a legacy project, comprising all of Jeff's teachings—an anthology of his years of experience and insights. And if there's one thing I've learned about Jeff, it's that his superpower truly is being a teacher. His ability to break down complex concepts, to make LinkedIn® "easy peasy" (as I like to say), is unparalleled.

As you read through these pages, you'll find more than just tips and tricks for LinkedIn® success. You'll find Jeff's warmth, his genuine desire to help others, and his unique ability to make everyone feel like they can conquer the professional world. From optimizing your profile to building meaningful connections, from creating engaging content to leveraging advanced features - it's all here, explained with Jeff's signature friendly style.

This book is my gift to Jeff as a thank you for his tireless service. But this book is also a gift to the entire LinkedIn® community – a comprehensive guide to being effective on LinkedIn®, accessible to all. It's a perfect reflection of Jeff's generous spirit, always taking what he receives and multiplying its impact for the benefit of others.

So, whether you're a LinkedIn® novice or a seasoned pro, prepare to dive in and learn from the best. Jeff's insights will not only help you navigate LinkedIn® more effectively but will also inspire you to approach your professional journey with authenticity, generosity, and a spirit of continuous learning.

Here's to Jeff Young, #TheLinkedInGuru, a teacher, a mentor, and a true friend to me and everyone else in the LinkedIn® community. May his wisdom in these pages help you unlock your full potential on LinkedIn® and beyond.

Gillian Whitney

Livestream & Author Brand Strategist

Chief Collaborator of Jeff Young (aka #TheLinkedInGuru)

Introduction

Hey there, LinkedIn® enthusiasts! Jeff Young here, but you might know me better as #TheLinkedInGuru. My network of friends gave me that "Guru" moniker. When you look "Guru" up in the dictionary you see the word "Teacher". Which perfectly represents my brand and is why I always say "I'm a Teacher... What's YOUR superpower"!

First off, a heartfelt thank you for picking up this book. I never thought when I started my LinkedIn® journey back in May 2004 that I'd be writing a book about it almost two decades later!

Now, you might be wondering, "Jeff, why should I listen to you about LinkedIn®?"

Well, let me tell you a story. I was one of the first 600,000 members to join LinkedIn® (member #594945 to be exact). Since then, I've been on quite the adventure, providing nearly 200 free LinkedIn® workshops in just the last 3 years. All told, I've been teaching LinkedIn® for 17 years now.

Do the math, and that's about 1,000 seminars with roughly 20 people per seminar.

That's over 20,000 people I've had the pleasure of helping – and that's not even counting the ripple effect!

But here's the thing, folks. LinkedIn® isn't just a website or an app. It's a powerful tool that, when used effectively, can supercharge your professional life. Whether you're a job seeker, an entrepreneur, or just looking to expand your professional network, LinkedIn® is where the magic happens.

In this book, we're going to dive into everything I've learned about being effective on LinkedIn®. We'll cover it all – from setting up a profile that would make your momma proud, to connecting with the right people (not just anyone who can "fog a mirror"), to participating in a way that adds value, not noise.

Remember, LinkedIn® is like a gym membership. If you never go to the gym (LinkedIn®) and you never put in the time to learn how to use the equipment (LinkedIn® features), then the gym (LinkedIn®) will probably not help you reach your goals. But don't worry – I'm here to be your personal LinkedIn® trainer!

We'll talk about the Three P's: Profile, People, and Participate. We'll discuss how to make your profile sing, how to build a network (not just a database), and how to engage in a way that's meaningful and effective.

Along the way, I'll share some of my favorite tips and tricks, like how to use Boolean search logic to find exactly who you're looking for, or how to leverage LinkedIn®'s Services Page to showcase what you offer.

Now, I don't EVER say that you HAVE to do it my way. I believe that "the best Teachers show you where to look… but they don't tell you what to see"!

What works for me might not work for you, and that's okay! LinkedIn® is beautiful because we can all approach it differently. But I can tell you that the approaches and things I'll share in this book have been very successful for me. I hope they'll help YOU be successful as well.

So, are you ready to become a LinkedIn® ninja? Great! Let's dive in and start our journey to LinkedIn® effectiveness together. Remember, on LinkedIn® (and in life), you get out what you put in. So let's put in the effort and reap the rewards!

Namaste and let's get started!

Chapter 1

Getting Started - The Foundations of LinkedIn® Success

Alright, folks, let's kick things off with the basics. You know, when I started on LinkedIn® way back in 2004, it was like stepping into a whole new world. Now, it's become as essential as your morning coffee (or tea, if that's your thing). So, let's talk about how to lay a solid foundation for your LinkedIn® success.

First Things First: Your Profile

Your LinkedIn® profile is where everything starts. It's like your digital handshake, your online business card, and your personal billboard all rolled into one. And let me tell you, you've got to make it sing!

Remember, you get 7-10 seconds when someone comes to your profile to get them to pay attention and STAY around. So, focus on what I call the "Big 5" areas:

1. Background Photo/Banner

2. Profile Photo (Headshot Picture)

3. Name

4. Professional Headline

5. About section

These are your prime real estate to differentiate yourself and "speak" to your tribe!

Now, here's a crucial tip: It's not all about YOU. I know, I know, it's your profile, but hear me out.

Your profile should speak to your customer, audience, prospect, or (dare I say it) TRIBE! Make it about what you can do for them, not just about your past accomplishments.

The LinkedIn® Ecosystem

LinkedIn® isn't just a website; it's a whole ecosystem. You've got your feed, your network, groups, company pages, and more. It's important to understand how all these pieces fit together.

One thing to keep in mind: LinkedIn® is always evolving. What worked yesterday might not work tomorrow. That's why it's crucial to stay up-to-date and be willing to adapt. Trust me, I've seen a lot of changes over the years!

The Three P's: Profile, People, Participate

Now, let's talk about what I call the Three P's of LinkedIn® success:

1. Profile: We've touched on this, but it bears repeating. Your profile is your story, and your story is your brand. Make it professional AND personal. Be proud of who you are, but humble enough to say, "No brag, just fact" about everything you include.

2. People: Connect with the RIGHT people, not just anyone who can "fog a mirror". Build relationships, not just a database. Remember, connecting is the BEGINNING of the process, not the END.

3. Participate: DO something good on LinkedIn®. Provide valuable content, not noise. Interact with your network by commenting and providing respectful feedback. And, above all, GIVE, GIVE, GIVE!

These Three P's are the secret sauce to being effective on LinkedIn®. Keep them in mind as we dive deeper in the coming chapters.

Getting in the LinkedIn® Mindset

Before we wrap up this chapter, let me share one last piece of advice: Approach LinkedIn® with the right mindset. It's not just about what you can get; it's about what you can give. Be curious, be helpful, be genuine.

Remember, LinkedIn® is a platform for professional growth and connection. It's not Facebook (save those cat videos for later), and it's not Twitter (no need for heated political debates here). It's a place where we can all learn from each other, support each other, and grow together.

So, are you ready to dive in and make LinkedIn® work for you? Great! In the next chapter, we'll get into the nitty-gritty of optimizing your profile. Trust me, it's going to be fun!

Namaste and see you in the next chapter!

Chapter 2

Optimizing Your LinkedIn® Profile

Alright, my LinkedIn® friends, let's dive into the meat and potatoes of your LinkedIn® presence – your profile. Think of your profile as your own personal billboard on the LinkedIn® highway. You want it to catch people's attention and make them want to pull over and learn more about you.

Make Your Profile Sing!

First things first, let's talk about completing your profile. LinkedIn® used to call this being an "All-Star", and while they might have changed the name, the concept is still crucial. Here's what you need to hit that 100% mark:

- Industry and Location
- Current Position
- Education section

- Profile Photo
- At least 50 connections
- A minimum of 5 skills
- About (Summary) section

But folks, let me tell you, just filling in the blanks isn't enough. We want to optimize, not just complete!

The Power of Keywords

Now, here's where we get into the secret sauce – keywords. If you want to be found, you've got to include the right keywords in the right places. It's like a game of hide and seek, except you want to be found!

Focus on including your most important keywords in these four key areas:

1. Your Professional Headline (you've got 220 characters, make 'em count!)
2. Your About section (weave those keywords into a compelling story)
3. Your Experience section (both in titles and descriptions)
4. Your Skills section (this is a goldmine for keywords)

Here's a pro tip: use Google Trends to check how popular your keyword phrases are. You might be surprised! I once discovered that "LinkedIn® Training" was searched 9 times more often than "LinkedIn® Trainer". Guess what? I updated my profile, and boom – my search appearances skyrocketed!

Visual Appeal Matters

Now, let's talk visuals. Your profile needs to look good too! Pay special attention to these areas:

1. Banner/Background Photo (show off your brand!)

2. Profile Photo (make it professional, but let your personality shine)

3. Featured section (showcase your best work)

Remember, you eat with your eyes first, and the same goes for LinkedIn® profiles!

Crafting Your Story

Your About section is where you get to tell your story. Make it conversational, make it engaging, and most importantly, make it about how you can help your audience.

Remember, the first 3-4 lines are crucial – that's all people see before they have to click "see more". Make those "front-loaded" lines count!

Recommendations and Endorsements

Last but not least, don't forget about recommendations and endorsements. These are like gold stars on your LinkedIn® report card. But here's the thing – don't just wait for them to come to you. Be proactive!

Give recommendations to others (I aim for two given for every one received), and don't be shy about asking for them in return. For endorsements, focus on your top skills – these are the ones that really matter.

Wrapping It Up

Remember, folks, your profile is never truly "complete". I've been at this for over 16 years, and I'm still tweaking and improving my profile. It's a living, breathing representation of your professional self. Keep it updated, keep it fresh, and most importantly, keep it authentically you.

Your LinkedIn® profile is your chance to shine. Don't just list your job titles and duties – show the world who you are, what you're passionate about, and how you can add value. Make it so compelling that when someone lands on your profile, they can't help but want to connect with you.

So, go ahead, take another look at your profile. Is it telling your story the way you want it to? Is it speaking to your tribe? If not, well, you know what to do!

Namaste and happy optimizing!

Chapter 3

Building Your Network

Alright, LinkedIn® pals, now that we've got your profile shining like a diamond, let's talk about one of the most important aspects of LinkedIn® – your network. After all, what's the point of being on a social network if you're not, well, networking?

Quality Over Quantity

First things first – let's bust a myth. The size of your network isn't everything. I've seen folks with thousands of connections who aren't getting any real value from LinkedIn®. Why? Because they're focused on quantity, not quality.

Remember, we're building a network, not a database. Connect with the RIGHT people, not just anyone who can "fog a mirror". Your goal should be to build relationships, not just collect connection numbers.

The Art of Connecting

When it comes to connecting, I like to follow a simple rule: connect with people you already know first. These are folks who are already part of your network and would return your phone call. Then, look for people you DON'T know but WANT to know.

Here's a little trick I use – I prefer to "follow" first before connecting. It gives you a chance to see their content and engage with them before taking it to the next level.

Personalize Your Invitations

Please, oh please, don't use the default "I'd like to add you to my professional network on LinkedIn®" message when sending connection requests. That's about as exciting as watching paint dry! Take a moment to write a personal note. Tell them why you want to connect, maybe mention something you have in common. Show them you've taken the time to look at their profile.

Engage, Engage, Engage!

Once you've connected, don't just let that connection gather dust. Engage with your network! Comment on their posts, congratulate them on their achievements, share their content if it's relevant to your audience. Remember, networking is a two-way street.

I always say, "You haven't connected until you have conversed". So start those conversations!

Supporting Your TRIBE

Now, let's talk about something I'm really passionate about – your LinkedIn® TRIBE (Together Really Is Better For Everyone). Supporting your tribe is crucial for LinkedIn® success. Here are some ways you can do that:

1. Like and comment on posts
2. Provide skill endorsements (but only for skills you can vouch for!)
3. Write thoughtful recommendations
4. Celebrate milestones and achievements
5. Stay in touch through direct messages
6. Make meaningful introductions
7. Create shout-out posts

Remember, "If you support your network, you will never spend a lonely day in your life."

The Power of Giving

Here's a little secret – the more you GIVE on LinkedIn®, the more you GET back. Seek first to help others.

Share your knowledge, offer support, make introductions. It might feel counterintuitive, but trust me, it works.

I have a goal of giving two recommendations for every one that I receive. When I see the ratio of given to received on a person's profile, it gives me an idea of what type of networker they really are.

Keeping Your Promises

Finally, let's talk about keeping your promises on LinkedIn®. When you connect with someone, you're making a promise to be a valuable part of their network. Here are some promises I make to my network:

- I promise to connect once we've "met" (either in person or through meaningful online interaction)
- I promise to thank you for interacting
- I promise to provide value
- I promise not to try to sell you anything (remember, I do what I do for free!)
- I promise to stay in touch

These promises help build trust and strengthen your relationships on LinkedIn®.

Wrapping It Up

Building a strong network on LinkedIn® isn't about collecting connections like Pokémon cards. It's about fostering genuine relationships, supporting others, and adding value to your professional community.

Remember, your network is your net worth. Treat it with care, nurture it, and watch it grow into a powerful resource that supports your professional journey.

So, go ahead and take a look at your network. Are you connecting with the right people? Are you engaging meaningfully? Are you supporting your TRIBE? If not, well, you know what to do!

Namaste and happy networking!

Chapter 4

Content Creation and Engagement

Alright, LinkedIn® rockstars, now that we've got your profile polished and your network growing, let's talk about the lifeblood of LinkedIn® – content and engagement. This is where the rubber really meets the road!

Quality Over Quantity (Again!)

First things first – let's address the elephant in the room. How often should you post? Well, I'm going to say something that might ruffle some feathers: don't post too often. I know, I know, you've probably heard that you should post every day, maybe even multiple times a day. But here's the thing – QUALITY and VALUE win over QUANTITY every time.

My advice? Post when you have something meaningful to say. Provide valuable content, not noise. Be consistent in both content and timing. Have a "theme" that you come back to often, like my "Tip of the Week" or "Monday Motivation".

When it comes to content on LinkedIn® I like to express it this way:

1. Content is King (you should contribute on subjects you know well)

2. Context is King Kong (if your content doesn't relate to you audience, you are just talking to yourself)

3. Consistency is King Kong's MOTHER! (consistently showing up and adding value trumps everything else when it comes to content)

The Art of Engagement

Now, here's a little secret – commenting is often more powerful than posting. I spend far more time commenting than I do posting. Why? Because that's where the real conversations happen. That's where relationships are built.

I aim for a ratio of about 10 comments for every post. It's not a hard and fast rule, but it's a good guideline. Remember, LinkedIn® is a social platform. Be social!

Types of Content That Work

So, what kind of content should you be sharing? Well, that depends on your goals and your audience. But here are some ideas:

1. Industry insights
2. How-to guides
3. Personal experiences and lessons learned
4. Thought leadership pieces
5. Celebratory posts (for your achievements or those of others)
6. Questions to spark discussion

And don't forget about LinkedIn®'s various content formats – posts, articles, documents, videos, and even newsletters.

Speaking of newsletters, if you're thinking about starting one, go for it! It's a great way to provide consistent value to your audience. Just make sure you're committed to publishing regularly.

Using Multimedia

Don't be afraid to mix things up with different types of media. Videos, images, and even audio can make your content more engaging. Just remember, if you're using audio or video, always provide captions. Many people browse LinkedIn® with the sound off, and we want to be inclusive of those with hearing difficulties.

The Power of Authenticity

Here's something crucial – be yourself. Your content should reflect your personality, your values, and your unique perspective. Don't try to be someone you're not. Authenticity is key on LinkedIn® (and in life!).

Engaging with Others' Content

Engagement isn't just about your own content. It's also about how you interact with others'. When you comment on someone's post, don't just say "Great post!" Add value to the conversation. Share your perspective, ask a question, or relate it to your own experience.

And here's a pet peeve of mine – don't ghost someone when they reply to YOUR comment. If they take the time to respond, acknowledge it. That's how real conversations happen!

The LinkedIn® Algorithm

Now, I know some folks get really hung up on the LinkedIn® algorithm. But here's my take – don't worry too much about it. Focus on creating valuable content and engaging genuinely, and the algorithm will take care of itself.

That said, there are a few things to keep in mind:

1. LinkedIn® favors native content (content posted directly on LinkedIn® rather than links to external sites)

2. Engagement in the first few hours after posting is crucial

3. Comments carry more weight than likes or other reactions

What NOT to Do

Before we wrap up, let's talk about a few things to avoid:

1. Don't join "engagement pods" – these groups artificially inflate engagement and can actually hurt you in the long run

2. Avoid "tag walls" – mentioning a bunch of people in your posts without their permission is just spammy

3. Don't use automation tools that violate LinkedIn®'s terms of service

4. Avoid posting and then ignoring the comments – engage with people who take the time to comment on your content

Wrapping It Up

Content creation and engagement on LinkedIn® is an art and a science. It takes time, effort, and a willingness to put yourself out there. But when done right, it can be incredibly rewarding.

Remember, the goal isn't just to get likes or comments. It's to provide value, start conversations, and build relationships. That's what LinkedIn® is all about.

So, take a look at your content strategy. Are you providing value? Are you engaging authentically? Are you being consistent? If not, well, you know what to do!

Namaste and happy posting!

Chapter 5

Advanced LinkedIn® Techniques

Alright, LinkedIn® ninjas, now that we've covered the basics, it's time to level up! In this chapter, we're going to dive into some advanced techniques that can really supercharge your LinkedIn® game. So, strap in and let's get technical!

Boolean Search Logic: Finding the Needle in the Haystack

First up, let's talk about Boolean search logic. Now, don't let the fancy name scare you off - it's actually pretty simple once you get the hang of it. Boolean searching allows you to combine words and phrases using AND, OR, and NOT to narrow down your search results.

Here's a quick example:

"headline: LinkedIn® AND skills: coaching AND NOT: job"

This search would find people with "LinkedIn®" in their headline, "coaching" in their skills, but who aren't currently looking for a job. Pretty nifty, right?

Remember, on a free account, you're limited to about 40 searches per month before LinkedIn® starts restricting your results. That's why targeted searches are so important!

Leveraging LinkedIn®'s Services Page

Next up, let's talk about the Services Page. This is a great free resource that LinkedIn® offers, especially useful for freelancers, entrepreneurs, and consultants.

To set up your Services Page, go to your profile and click on the "Open to" button, then select "Providing Services". You can list the services you offer, provide a description, and even allow people to request proposals from you.

Here's a pro tip: once you've set up your Services Page, you can invite up to 20 connections per year to review your services. These reviews can be a great way to build credibility and attract new clients.

Utilizing External Tools

Now, let's talk about some external tools that can help boost your LinkedIn® game. Two of my favorites are Canva and Google Trends.

Canva is great for creating eye-catching graphics for your posts and banner images. It's user-friendly and has tons of templates specifically designed for LinkedIn®.

Google Trends, on the other hand, can help you choose the best keywords for your profile. For example, I once discovered that "LinkedIn® Training" was searched 9 times more often than "LinkedIn® Trainer". After updating my profile with this insight, my search appearances skyrocketed!

Mastering LinkedIn® Settings and Privacy Options

Last but definitely not least, let's talk about settings and privacy. Did you know there are hundreds of different settings you can adjust on LinkedIn®? Yep, you read that right! This is an area that I highly recommend you delve into and figure out what each of these settings means because it will help you control how YOU interact with LinkedIn®. If you take more control, then you will be more effective. It's as simple as that!

Some key areas to focus on:

1. Profile visibility: Decide who can see your full profile, your connections, etc.

2. Active status: Choose whether people can see when you're online.

3. Data privacy: Control how LinkedIn® uses your

data and who can download your contact info. Data privacy is also where you can "Get a copy of your data". It is extremely important to download a backup of your data frequently because you are building your profile on "rented ground".

4. Communication preferences: Manage how you receive notifications and messages.

One setting I highly recommend is turning on two-step verification. It's a simple way to add an extra layer of security to your account.

Also, don't forget to regularly check where you're signed in from. It's a good habit to sign out of any sessions you don't recognize and consider changing your password if something looks fishy.

Wrapping It Up

These advanced techniques can really take your LinkedIn® presence to the next level. They allow you to find exactly who you're looking for, showcase your services more effectively, create more engaging content, and keep your account secure.

Remember, LinkedIn® is always evolving, so it's important to stay curious and keep learning. What works today might not work tomorrow, so don't be afraid to experiment and adapt your strategy.

So, LinkedIn® superstars, are you ready to put these advanced techniques into practice? Remember, with great power comes great responsibility. Use these tools wisely, and always with the intention of adding value to your network.

Namaste and happy advanced LinkedIn®-ing!

Chapter 6

LinkedIn® for Specific Goals

Alright, LinkedIn® champions, now that we've covered the advanced stuff, let's talk about how to tailor your LinkedIn® strategy for specific goals. Whether you're job hunting, building your personal brand, generating leads, or aiming for thought leadership, LinkedIn® can be your secret weapon. Let's dive in!

Job Seeking on LinkedIn®

If you're on the hunt for a new gig, LinkedIn® is your best friend. Here's how to make the most of it:

1. Turn on "Open to Work": This lets recruiters know you're available. You can choose to show this to everyone (with a special "Open to Work" frame) or just recruiters.

2. Use your headline wisely: Instead of just your current job title, use this space to highlight your skills and what you're looking for. For example: "Marketing Specialist, SEO Expert, Seeking New Opportu-

nities in Digital Marketing"

3. Optimize for keywords: Remember what we talked about in Chapter 2? Make sure your profile is loaded with the right keywords for the jobs you want.

4. Engage with target companies: Follow companies you're interested in, comment on their posts, and connect with people who work there.

5. Use LinkedIn® Jobs: Set up job alerts and take advantage of the "Easy Apply" feature when available.

Remember, your network is your net worth when job seeking. Don't be shy about letting your connections know you're looking!

Personal Branding

For those of you looking to build a strong personal brand, LinkedIn® is your stage. Here's how to shine:

1. Consistency is key: Make sure your profile, posts, and comments all align with your personal brand.

2. Share your expertise: Post regularly about your area of expertise. Think "how-to" posts, industry insights, and lessons learned.

3. Show your personality: Don't be afraid to let your unique voice shine through. Be professional, but be

you!

4. Engage authentically: Comment on others' posts, share interesting content, and be a positive force in your network.

5. Use rich media: Take advantage of LinkedIn®'s features like images and video to bring your brand to life.

Business Development and Lead Generation

If you're using LinkedIn® for lead gen, here's how to make it work for you:

1. Optimize your profile for your target audience: Make sure your profile speaks directly to the problems you solve for your ideal clients.

2. Use LinkedIn® Sales Navigator or a Business Account on LinkedIn®: If your budget allows, these tools can supercharge your lead gen efforts.

3. Provide value first: Share helpful content, offer insights, and build relationships before trying to sell.

4. Leverage your network for introductions: Remember, a warm introduction is always better than a cold outreach.

5. Use LinkedIn®'s Services Page: We talked about

this in Chapter 5. It's a great way to showcase what you offer.

Thought Leadership

Want to position yourself as a thought leader in your industry? Here's how:

1. Consistency is crucial: Regularly share insights, predictions, and analysis about your industry.

2. Start conversations: Don't just share your thoughts - ask questions and encourage discussion.

3. Write long-form articles: Use LinkedIn®'s article feature to dive deep into topics.

4. Engage with other thought leaders: Comment on and share content from others in your field.

5. Consider starting a LinkedIn® Newsletter: This can be a great and powerful way to regularly share your insights with your audience.

Remember, becoming a thought leader doesn't happen overnight. It takes time, consistency, and a willingness to put your ideas out there.

Wrapping It Up

No matter what your goal is on LinkedIn®, remember this: it's not about gaming the system or tricking the algorithm.

It's about providing value, building genuine relationships, and consistently showing up as your best professional self.

Your LinkedIn® strategy should be as unique as you are. Take these tips and adapt them to fit your personality, your industry, and your specific goals.

And here's a final piece of advice: don't be afraid to pivot. If something's not working, try a different approach. LinkedIn® is always evolving, and so should your strategy.

So, LinkedIn® superstars, are you ready to crush your goals? Remember, whether you're job seeking, brand building, lead generating, or thought leading, LinkedIn® is your playground. Make the most of it!

Namaste and may all your LinkedIn® goals come true!

Chapter 7

Measuring Your LinkedIn® Success

Alright, LinkedIn® champions, we've covered a lot of ground so far. But here's the million-dollar question: How do you know if all your hard work is paying off? That's where measuring your LinkedIn® success comes in. Let's dive into the world of LinkedIn® analytics and metrics!

Understanding LinkedIn® Analytics

First things first, let's talk about where to find your analytics. If you're using a personal profile, you can find some basic stats under your profile view. For more detailed info, look for the "Analytics" area (sometimes referred to as a "Dashboard" on your profile. If you're using a Company Page, you'll find a wealth of data under the "Analytics" tab there as well.

Key Metrics to Track

Now, what should you be looking at? Here are some key metrics I always keep an eye on:

1. Profile Views: This tells you how many people are checking out your profile. If this number is going up, you're doing something right!

2. Search Appearances: This shows you how many times you've shown up in LinkedIn® searches. Remember those keywords we talked about? This is where they really come into play.

3. Post Views: This gives you an idea of how many people are seeing your content.

4. Engagement Rate: This is the percentage of people who interact with your posts (likes, comments, shares) compared to how many saw it. Quality beats quantity here, folks!

5. Connection Growth: Keep track of how your network is growing over time.

Remember, these numbers aren't just vanity metrics. They're valuable insights into how you're performing on the platform.

Digging Deeper into Your Data

Now, let's get a bit more granular:

1. Who's Viewing Your Profile: LinkedIn® gives you some info about who's checking you out. Are they in your industry? Are they from companies you're targeting? This can give you great insights.

2. Content Performance: Look at which of your posts are performing best. What topics resonate? What formats (text, image, video) get the most engagement?

3. Follower Demographics: Understanding who's following you can help you tailor your content more effectively.

4. Best Times to Post: LinkedIn® can show you when your audience is most active. Use this to time your posts for maximum impact.

Adjusting Your Strategy Based on Results

Here's where the rubber meets the road. Once you've got all this data, what do you do with it? Here are some ways to use your analytics to improve your LinkedIn® game:

1. Double down on what works: If certain types of posts are getting great engagement, do more of those!

2. Experiment with timing: Try posting at different times based on when your audience is most active.

3. Refine your keywords: If your search appearances

are low, it might be time to revisit your keyword strategy.

4. Expand your network strategically: If you're not reaching the right people, use your follower demographics to guide your connection strategy.

5. Improve your content mix: If your engagement rate is low, try mixing up your content types. Maybe throw in a poll or a video to shake things up.

Don't Get Obsessed with Numbers

Now, here's an important caveat: while these metrics are valuable, don't get too caught up in the numbers game. Remember, LinkedIn® is about building relationships and providing value. A smaller, highly engaged network is often more valuable than a large, disengaged one.

As I always say, "You get out of LinkedIn® what you put into LinkedIn®." Focus on consistently providing value, engaging authentically, and building real relationships. The numbers will follow.

Wrapping It Up

Measuring your LinkedIn® success isn't about hitting arbitrary numbers. It's about understanding how effectively you're reaching and engaging with your target audience, and using that information to continually improve your LinkedIn® strategy.

So, LinkedIn® superstars, are you ready to dive into your analytics? Remember, knowledge is power. Use these insights to refine your approach, but never lose sight of the real goal: building meaningful professional relationships.

Namaste and happy number crunching!

Chapter 8

Staying Up-to-Date with LinkedIn®

Alright, my LinkedIn® dynamos, we've covered a lot of ground in this book. But here's the thing about LinkedIn® – it's always changing! Just when you think you've got it all figured out, they roll out a new feature or tweak the algorithm. So in this chapter, let's talk about how to stay on top of your LinkedIn® game.

Keep Your Finger on the Pulse

First things first, how do you keep up with all these changes? Here are a few strategies I swear by:

1. Follow LinkedIn®'s Official Blog: This is where they announce major updates and new features.

2. Join relevant LinkedIn® Groups for Professionals: There are plenty of groups out there dedicated to discussing LinkedIn® strategies. Join a few and participate in the conversations.

3. Follow LinkedIn® Experts: There are folks out there (like yours truly) who make it their business to stay on top of LinkedIn® trends. Follow them and pay attention to what they're saying.

4. Experiment, Experiment, Experiment: Don't be afraid to try out new features as soon as they're released. You might just discover the next big thing before everyone else!

Adapting to Algorithm Changes

Now, let's talk about the elephant in the room – the LinkedIn® algorithm. It's constantly evolving, and what worked yesterday might not work tomorrow. Here's how to roll with the punches:

1. Focus on Engagement: No matter how the algorithm changes, genuine engagement is always valued. Keep creating content that sparks conversations.

2. Watch Your Analytics: If you notice sudden changes in your reach or engagement, it might be due to an algorithm update. Don't panic – adjust your strategy and keep moving forward.

3. Diversify Your Content: Don't put all your eggs in one basket. Mix up your content types (text, images, videos, polls) to see what resonates best with your audience and the current algorithm.

Continuous Learning and Improvement

Here's a little secret – even after all these years on LinkedIn®, I'm still learning every day. Here's how you can keep improving your LinkedIn® game:

1. Take LinkedIn®'s Free Courses: LinkedIn® Learning offers courses on how to use the platform effectively. Take advantage of them!

2. Attend LinkedIn® Events: Whether they're online or in-person, LinkedIn® events can be great places to learn new strategies and network with other professionals.

3. Ask for Feedback: Don't be afraid to ask your network how you're doing. What do they like about your content? What could you improve?

4. Learn from Your Competitors: Keep an eye on what other successful people in your industry are doing on LinkedIn®. What can you learn from them?

Embracing New Features

LinkedIn® is always rolling out new features. Remember when they introduced LinkedIn® Live? Or how about when they launched Newsletters? Here's my advice – embrace these new features early. They often get a boost in the algorithm, and early adopters can really stand out.

But remember, don't just use a new feature because it's new. Make sure it aligns with your overall LinkedIn® strategy and goals.

The Future of LinkedIn®

Now, I'm no fortune teller, but I've been around long enough to see some trends. Here's what I think we'll see more of on LinkedIn® in the coming years:

1. More Visual Content: Think short-form videos, media posts, and interactive content.

2. Increased Focus on Personal Branding: LinkedIn® is becoming more and more about individual voices, not just company pages.

3. AI-Powered Features: We're already seeing this with things like LinkedIn®'s automated job matches. Expect more AI integration in the future.

4. Greater Emphasis on Skills: LinkedIn® is already moving towards skills-based hiring. This trend is likely to continue.

Wrapping It Up

Staying up-to-date with LinkedIn® isn't about chasing every new trend or feature. It's about being adaptable, staying curious, and always focusing on providing value to your network.

Remember, at its core, LinkedIn® is about building professional relationships. No matter how the platform changes, that fundamental truth will remain the same.

So, my LinkedIn® superstars, are you ready to evolve with LinkedIn®? Remember, the only constant is change. Embrace it, learn from it, and use it to your advantage.

Namaste and here's to your continued LinkedIn® success!

Chapter 9

Common Mistakes to Avoid on LinkedIn®

Alright, LinkedIn® champions, we've covered a lot of ground on what you should do to be effective on LinkedIn®. But let's flip the script and talk about what NOT to do. After all, sometimes knowing what to avoid is just as important as knowing what to pursue. So, let's dive into some common LinkedIn® pitfalls and how to steer clear of them!

The "Connect and Pitch" Syndrome

First up, let's talk about a pet peeve of mine - the dreaded "connect and pitch" approach. You know what I'm talking about - someone connects with you and immediately tries to sell you something. Don't be that person!

Remember, LinkedIn® is about building relationships, not making a quick sale. Take the time to engage with your new connections. Comment on their posts, congratulate them on their achievements, and add value before you even think about pitching anything.

Oversharing Personal Information

Now, I'm all for being authentic on LinkedIn®, but there's a line between professional authenticity and oversharing. LinkedIn® isn't Facebook or Instagram. Your network probably doesn't need to know what you had for breakfast or see pictures from your wild weekend.

Keep it professional, folks. Share personal anecdotes when they're relevant to your professional life or when they add value to your network. But always ask yourself, "Would I be comfortable with my boss or a potential client seeing this?"

Neglecting Your Profile

We talked a lot about optimizing your profile in earlier chapters, but it bears repeating - don't let your profile gather dust! Your LinkedIn® profile isn't a "set it and forget it" kind of thing. It needs regular care and feeding.

Make it a habit to review and update your profile regularly. Add new skills you've acquired, update your experience, and refresh your About section. Keep it current, folks!

Ignoring LinkedIn®'s Features

LinkedIn® is constantly rolling out new features, and I see too many people ignoring them. Whether it's LinkedIn® Live, Newsletters, or the Services Page, these features are opportunities to stand out and engage with your network in new ways.

Don't be afraid to experiment with new features. You might just find a new favorite way to connect with your audience!

Automation Overload

Now, I know we're all busy, and automation tools can be tempting. But be careful! Over-automation can make you seem robotic and impersonal. And some automation tools violate LinkedIn®'s terms of service, which could get you in hot water.

Remember, LinkedIn® is about genuine connections. Don't sacrifice authenticity for convenience.

The "Post and Ghost" Phenomenon

Here's another one that grinds my gears - posting content and then disappearing. If someone takes the time to comment on your post, engage with them! Reply to comments, thank people for sharing, and keep the conversation going.

Engagement is a two-way street, folks. Don't just broadcast - participate!

Inconsistency

Consistency is key on LinkedIn®. I see too many people posting like crazy for a week and then disappearing for a month. Or connecting with lots of people and then never engaging with their network.

Remember, building your LinkedIn® presence is a marathon, not a sprint. It's better to post quality content once a week consistently than to post daily for a short burst and then vanish.

Ignoring LinkedIn® Etiquette

Every platform has its own etiquette, and LinkedIn® is no exception. Here are a few LinkedIn® faux pas to avoid:

1. Don't use all caps - it's the digital equivalent of shouting.

2. Avoid controversial topics unless they're directly related to your professional field.

3. Don't tag people in posts without their permission.

4. Respect people's time - keep your messages concise and to the point.

Focusing Too Much on Vanity Metrics

While it's great to see your follower count or post views go up, don't get too caught up in these vanity metrics. Remember, it's about quality, not quantity. A smaller, engaged network is much more valuable than a large, disinterested one.

Focus on meaningful engagement and building real relationships, not just pumping up your numbers.

Wrapping It Up

Remember, we all make mistakes - I certainly have over my years on LinkedIn®. The key is to learn from them and keep improving. If you catch yourself making any of these mistakes, don't beat yourself up. Just course correct and move forward.

LinkedIn® is a powerful tool when used correctly. By avoiding these common pitfalls, you'll be well on your way to LinkedIn® success.

So, LinkedIn® superstars, are you ready to navigate the LinkedIn® landscape with confidence? Remember, every mistake is an opportunity to learn and grow. Here's to your continued success on LinkedIn®!

Namaste and happy LinkedIn®-ing!

Chapter 10

Conclusion - Your LinkedIn® Journey Continues

Well, LinkedIn® champions, we've come to the end of our journey through this book, but remember - your LinkedIn® journey is just beginning (or continuing)! Let's take a moment to recap what we've learned and look ahead to your bright LinkedIn® future.

Key Takeaways

1. Your Profile is Your Foundation: We started with optimizing your profile because it's the cornerstone of your LinkedIn® presence. Remember, it's not just a resume - it's your professional story.

2. Networking is About Quality, Not Quantity: Focus on building meaningful connections, not just collecting them like Pokémon cards.

3. Content is King, Engagement is Queen: Consistently share valuable content, but don't forget to engage with others. It's a two-way street, folks!

4. Advanced Techniques Can Set You Apart: From Boolean search to leveraging the Services Page, these advanced techniques can give you an edge.

5. Tailor Your Approach to Your Goals: Whether you're job seeking, building your brand, or generating leads, LinkedIn® can be customized to fit your needs.

6. Measure, Analyze, Adjust: Keep an eye on your analytics and be willing to pivot your strategy when needed.

7. Stay Up-to-Date: LinkedIn® is always evolving, so stay curious and be willing to adapt.

8. Avoid Common Pitfalls: By steering clear of the mistakes we discussed, you'll be ahead of the game.

The LinkedIn® Mindset

Now, here's something I want you to take to heart - success on LinkedIn® isn't just about tactics and strategies. It's about adopting the right mindset. Here's what I mean:

1. Be Authentic: Don't try to be someone you're not. Your unique voice and perspective are your greatest assets.

2. Be Generous: Give more than you take. Share your knowledge, offer help, make introductions.

3. Be Curious: Never stop learning. There's always something new to discover on LinkedIn®.

4. Be Patient: Building a strong LinkedIn® presence takes time. Don't get discouraged if you don't see results overnight.

5. Be Consistent: Show up regularly, engage consistently, and keep providing value.

Your Next Steps

So, what should you do next? Here are some actionable steps to take:

1. Review Your Profile: Go through your profile with fresh eyes. Is it telling your story the way you want it to?

2. Set LinkedIn® Goals: What do you want to achieve on LinkedIn® in the next 3 months? 6 months? Year?

3. Create a Content Calendar: Plan out your content strategy. What will you share? How often?

4. Engage Daily: Make it a habit to spend at least 15 minutes a day engaging with your network.

5. Experiment with a New Feature: Try out something new, whether it's LinkedIn® Live, Newsletters, or polls.

6. Measure Your Progress: Set up a system to track your LinkedIn® metrics regularly.

Remember, You're Not Alone

One of the beautiful things about LinkedIn® is the community. You're not on this journey alone. Reach out to your network, join LinkedIn® groups, engage with thought leaders in your industry. Learn from others and don't be afraid to share your own insights.

A Personal Note

Before we wrap up, I want to share something personal. When I joined LinkedIn® back in 2004 (member #594945!), I had no idea where this journey would take me. But by consistently showing up, providing value, and building genuine relationships, I've been able to build a community that I'm truly grateful for.

And let me tell you, if I can do it, so can you. It doesn't matter if you're just starting out or if you've been on LinkedIn® for years. There's always room to grow, to learn, to connect.

Final Thoughts

LinkedIn® isn't just a platform - it's a community of professionals from all walks of life, all around the world. It's a place where you can learn, grow, and make meaningful connections that can transform your career and your life.

So, my LinkedIn® superstars, are you ready to take your LinkedIn® presence to the next level? Remember, every post, every comment, every connection is an opportunity to make an impact. Use it wisely, use it authentically, and watch the magic happen.

Thank you for coming along on this journey with me. I can't wait to see what you'll achieve on LinkedIn®. Remember, I'm rooting for you!

Namaste and here's to your LinkedIn® success!

Chapter 11

Appendices

Alright, LinkedIn® superstars, we've covered a lot of ground in this book. But before we wrap things up completely, I want to leave you with some handy resources that you can refer back to as you continue your LinkedIn® journey. Think of these appendices as your LinkedIn® cheat sheets!

Appendix A: LinkedIn® Etiquette Guide

1. Personalize connection requests: Always add a note explaining why you want to connect.

2. Respond to messages promptly: Even if it's just to say you'll get back to them later.

3. Give credit where it's due: If you share someone else's content, mention them.

4. Be respectful of people's time: Keep messages concise and to the point.

5. Don't spam: Avoid mass messaging your connec-

tions with sales pitches.

6. Engage authentically: Comment on posts with genuine insights, not just "Great post!"

7. Be professional: Remember, LinkedIn® is not Facebook. Keep it work-appropriate.

8. Ask before tagging: Don't tag people in posts without their permission.

9. Congratulate and celebrate: Acknowledge your connections' achievements.

10. Be helpful: If you can assist someone in your network, do it without expecting anything in return.

Appendix B: Glossary of LinkedIn® Terms

1. InMail: LinkedIn®'s internal messaging system that allows you to contact people you're not connected with (requires a Premium account).

2. Endorsements: Skills that your connections can vouch for on your profile.

3. Recommendations: Written testimonials on your profile from your connections.

4. Company Page: A LinkedIn® page for businesses and organizations.

5. Showcase Page: An extension of your Company

Page that highlights a specific brand, business unit, or initiative.

6. LinkedIn® Groups: Communities of professionals with similar interests.

7. LinkedIn® Learning: LinkedIn®'s online learning platform (formerly Lynda.com).

8. LinkedIn® Premium: Paid LinkedIn® accounts with additional features.

9. LinkedIn® Sales Navigator: LinkedIn®'s paid sales tool for lead generation and sales management.

Appendix C: Recommended Resources and Tools

1. LinkedIn® Learning: For courses on how to use LinkedIn® effectively.

2. Canva: For creating eye-catching graphics for your posts and profile.

3. Google Trends: For researching popular keywords to use in your profile.

4. Grammarly: To ensure your posts and profile are error-free.

5. Hootsuite or Buffer: For scheduling LinkedIn® posts (remember, authenticity is key!).

6. LinkedIn®'s Official Blog: To stay up-to-date with the latest LinkedIn® features and updates.

7. LinkedIn® Help Center: For troubleshooting and learning about specific LinkedIn® features.

8. LinkedIn® Salary: To research salary information for different roles and locations.

9. LinkedIn® Events: To find and host professional events.

10. LinkedIn® Newsletters: To share regular insights with your followers.

Appendix D: Quick LinkedIn® Profile Checklist

- Professional profile photo
- Eye-catching background image
- Compelling headline (remember those keywords!)
- Detailed "About" section that tells your professional story
- Complete work experience with achievements, not just responsibilities
- Education details
- Skills (at least 5, but aim for more)

- Volunteer experience (if applicable)
- Accomplishments (publications, patents, courses, projects, etc.)
- Recommendations (both given and received)
- Custom URL

Appendix E: LinkedIn® Content Ideas

1. Industry news and your take on it.
2. Behind-the-scenes looks at your work.
3. Tips and how-tos related to your expertise.
4. Career milestones and lessons learned.
5. Book recommendations.
6. Inspiring quotes (but add your own thoughts!).
7. Polls to engage your audience.
8. Client success stories (with permission).
9. Answers to frequently asked questions in your field.
10. Personal anecdotes that relate to your professional life.

Wrapping It Up

There you have it, folks! These appendices should serve as quick reference guides as you continue to build your LinkedIn® presence. Remember, LinkedIn® success doesn't happen overnight. It's about consistent effort, genuine engagement, and always providing value to your network.

Keep these resources handy, but don't forget the most important resource of all - your own unique perspective and experiences. That's what will truly set you apart on LinkedIn®.

So, LinkedIn® champions, are you ready to put all of this into practice? Remember, I'm rooting for you every step of the way. Now go out there and show LinkedIn® what you're made of!

Namaste and here's to your continued LinkedIn® success!

About the Author

Jeff Young, widely known as #TheLinkedInGuru, is a seasoned professional with over three decades of experience in education, performance development, and project management. His expertise is entirely his own, cultivated through years of practical experience and a passion for helping others succeed.

With more than 30 years in program design and delivery, and over 35 years in engagement and project management, Jeff has honed his skills in identifying organizational needs and developing tailored training programs for all levels of personnel. His career has been marked by significant contributions to improving business performance, productivity, quality, and profitability across various organizations.

Jeff's professional journey includes serving as a Director and Account Manager with Intellinex, an eLearning venture of Ernst & Young, LLP, where he helped manage and mentor thousands of individuals. His last corporate role was as an Enterprise Project Manager at OCLC, after which he transitioned into community service, volunteering for and helping manage several local non-profit organizations.

Since his retirement, Jeff has dedicated himself to being a Professional Networker and LinkedIn® trainer. He has trained thousands of professionals in maximizing their networking skills and utilizing networking tools effectively. His specialties include networking, social networking, LinkedIn® training, project management, eLearning, and management consulting.

Jeff's approach to LinkedIn® training is unique and hands-on. He offers free LinkedIn® seminars and workshops, believing in the power of giving back to the community. His Featured Section on LinkedIn® showcases examples of his presentations and provides valuable tips on how to use the platform effectively.

With his wealth of experience and his commitment to helping others, Jeff Young continues to be a respected voice in the world of professional networking and LinkedIn® optimization. His friendly, approachable style and deep knowledge make him a sought-after trainer and mentor for professionals looking to enhance their LinkedIn® presence and networking skills.

Connect with Jeff Young:

linkedin.com/in/jeffyoungralemoi/

Acknowledgments

A special thank you to Devon Whitney for his role in bringing this book to life. As Gillian Whitney's spouse and business partner, Devon ensured my work was presented professionally through layout and typesetting as well as navigating Amazon's self-publishing process for both Kindle and paperback formats.

Also, since much of the content for this book has come from my LinkedIn® Newsletters, I want to send a special thank you to the folks who have collaborated on that content: Stella Da Silva, Craig Langley, Jim Woolfe, and Gillian Whitney.

To those folks that have offered me a consistent forum to teach LinkedIn®, I extend my heartfelt thanks.

First, to Ken Lazar. I have known Ken for over 20 years, and for the last 10 plus years, he and I have been doing a "Stump the Guru" session as a part of his excellent Tuesday Tune-Up meetings for job seekers. We have done over 110 different seminars together.

Also, to Malka Bendor. She has been my "Jewish Mother" for nearly 10 years now, and we have done over 85 different sessions for her Jewish Family Services community of job seekers.

Thank you also to a special group of LinkedIn® peeps that I have never met in person but have come to rely on for their advice both on and off LinkedIn®:

Thank you to John Espirian, "the relentlessly helpful LinkedIn® nerd," who has been a shining inspiration ever since we connected in November 2018. One of my goals is to be as much like John as possible "when I grow up"!

Thank you to Kevin D. Turner, "the King of What's New" on LinkedIn®, for shining the light on all its many new features and for being a part of my "LinkedIn® Justice League" team for the last six plus years.

Thank you to Tiina Jarvet for truly living up to her brand of being a "Headhunter on your side" and collaborating with me on several workshops over the last five years. Tiina is one of the smartest people I know. She speaks 9 languages! She is also one of the most knowledgeable people on the planet about how to use LinkedIn® to show up in a Recruiter's search.

Thank you to Craig Allan (The Black Knight), who is actually one of the "Brightest Knights" I know and who shares my philosophy of Leadership and management style. Thank you for sharing your abundant heart with me and being a friend for these last five years.

Thank you to Angus Grady, my Empress Grey tea-drinking friend from across the pond for the last seven years, for always teaching me that "old school" can be today's "new school" and for inspirational quotes such as "Your connections don't have to add up. They just have to COUNT"!

Thank you to Debbie Wemyss, a fellow LinkedIn® Advocate, for her constant support over the last five years and for being such a great Teacher. She and I agree that teaching should be a combination of knowledge, guidance, and humor.

And thank you to Shelly Elsliger, my "sister from another mister" for the last seven years, who was the first person I met on LinkedIn® that I ever shared Christmas gifts with. We've built a special long-distance relationship that even includes buying each other many sets of matching T-shirts!

And finally, to my TRIBE of followers and connections on LinkedIn®, I say thank you for all your years of support. I thank you for making this the best online community in the world and for coming along on my 20-year journey. They say your "vibe attracts your tribe," and I believe it is true. I couldn't have come this far without you all. THANK YOU!

Printed in Great Britain
by Amazon

48910920R00046